Dick Bruna

Snuffy

Big Tent Entertainment

New York

D1058901

Snuffy is a nice brown puppy

with eyes as black as coal.

She likes to help and do good things,

for that is her one true goal.

When Snuffy, one fine morning,

looked through the window here,

she saw a little woman who

had shed a single tear.

Snuffy was so sad to see her,

and asked, "What's wrong with you?"

"I can't find my daughter,

and I don't know what to do."

"Oh, no," said Snuffy, "Oh, no.

That's sad news to hear.

Perhaps one of the animals

has seen her somewhere near."

Snuffy asked the snail first.

She said, "I wonder where . . ."

The snail said, "I am sorry.

I have not seen anyone here."

Then she asked the sparrows.

"Please tell me, birds," said she . . .

"No, Snuffy, we saw no one

from up here in our tree."

Snuffy asked the rabbit next,

"Have you seen a little child?"

"Oh, no. I've been in my hole

and haven't seen anyone in a while."

"What's that sound?" thought Snuffy.

"What is it that I hear?

Could it be that the little girl

is somewhere very near?"

And sure enough, a short way off,

there sat the sad little lass.

"I'm lost," she said to Snuffy,

and stood up from the grass.

"I finally found you!" said Snuffy.

"There's no need to be sad.

We'll run home together.

Your mother will be glad."

"Thank you, Snuffy," the woman said.

"You really are a dear.

You have found my daughter

and I'm very glad she's here."

After all that running

Snuffy needed a nap.

So the little girl gave Snuffy a hug

and held her in her lap.

Big Tent Entertainment
111 East 14th Street, #127
New York, NY 10003

Originally published in 1969 as *snuffie* by Mercis Publishing bv, Amsterdam, Netherlands.
Original text Dick Bruna © copyright Mercis Publishing bv, 1969.
Illustrations Dick Bruna © copyright Mercis bv, 1969.

Published in the U.S. in 2003 by Big Tent Entertainment, New York.
Publication licensed by Mercis Publishing bv, Amsterdam, through Big Tent Entertainment.
English translation © copyright 2003 by Mercis Publishing bv.

ISBN: 1-59226-028-4
Library of Congress Control Number: 2002113029

Printed in Germany.

10 9 8 7 6 5 4 3 2 1